High Explosive

FELIX BRUNNER'S LETTERS FROM THE
WESTERN FRONT

HUGO BRUNNER AND ANNE DYER

THE PERPETUA PRESS

OXFORD

First published in the United Kingdom
by The Perpetua Press in 2021
26 Norham Road OX2 6SF

ISBN 978-1-870882-21-7

Designed by Nicholas Clarke
and typeset in the United Kingdom
Printed and bound at the Holywell Press
Oxford

Front cover; 2nd Lt F J M Brunner RFA by Sir (Samuel) Luke Fildes, painted in
1917 Courtesy National Trust Images

DEDICATION

In memory of those who fought
and those who fell

CONTENTS

LIST OF ILLUSTRATIONS

The Brunner Family and the Great War

1 Sir John Tomlinson Brunner 1842-1919, MP, Pro-Chancellor of the University of Liverpool 1909-1918, by Arthur Hacker. *Courtesy Victoria Gallery and Museum, Liverpool*

2 Brunner Mond advertisement circa 1891. *Courtesy Grace's Guide to British Industrial History*

3 John Fletcher Moulton, 1st Baron Moulton. Image by Walter Stoneman 1917. *Courtesy National Portrait Gallery*

4 The Venesta factory, which produced wood veneer packing cases for the tea trade, in ruins following the detonation of TNT at the Brunner Mond explosives works in Silvertown, East London in January 1917. *@IWM (Q15364)*

5 Mrs Ethel J Blyth M.B.E. Commandant of The Grange Auxiliary Hospital, Chertsey 1915-1919. *Courtesy Lord Blyth*

Felix Brunner's War

1 Felix (middle row, third from right) aged 17 pictured with his house rugby team. *Courtesy Cheltenham College Archives*

2 Instructions to report to St John's Wood barracks. Extract from Felix Brunner's Service Record. *Courtesy The National Archives*

3 Excerpt from the war diary of 112th Brigade Royal Field Artillery recording Felix Brunner's arrival. *Courtesy The National Archives*

4 Royal Field Artillery 18 pounder battery preparing to open fire near Meteren 13 April 1918. Image by 2nd Lieut. David McLellan. *@IWM (Q8712)*

5 Operating Order issued to Felix's battery. Found in a collection of his papers and artefacts. *Courtesy Anne Dyer*

6 Position of Hill 63 and the changing British front lines as the battle progressed June 7 - June 11, 1917. *Taken from the Michelin Guide to the Ypres Battlefield pub. 1920, with thanks to Nick Champion*

7 German trench on Messines Ridge 7 June 1917. Image by Lieut. John Warwick Brooke. *@IWM (Q5787)*

The Rest of the Story

INTRODUCTION

MY father didn't talk much about his service in the First World War, at least not to my brothers and me. We were familiar with, and relished, the German military gear, now lodged at the Soldiers of Oxfordshire Museum in Woodstock, with which he had come home. The silver salver which the officers in his battery gave him when he got married in 1926 was also a familiar object. We were aware too of his regular attendance at dinners of the officers of the 29th Division – they came to an end when their number was reduced to seven. But towards the end of his life, in the seventies, he mentioned to me the letters which he wrote to his parents Jack and Lucy and his sister Joyce. Written in pencil in a fine hand, they survive in four ring-binders, together with an introduction which he wrote with my encouragement. It began: *'After an abortive attempt at the navy I decided to try for a commission in the Field Artillery. This was undoubtedly due to the help and encouragement of a new member of my mother's family, Colonel Edward Hall Stevenson, R.A. (1872-1964), who married my mother's double first cousin and very close friend'.*

I didn't do more than dip into these typed letters until 2008 when I received a call from the Canadian makers of a film in which he was to be the central figure, *A Secret Trench* (mentioned in this book). This got me excited. I read the letters several times. Then I visited Ypres and its neighbourhood with my brother Barnabas.

Felix was seen by his Oxford friends as having a humorous side to his personality. After reading some of these letters in November 1917 his grandfather, Sir John Tomlinson Brunner, wrote to his son Jack and remarked that *'his high spirits are a joy'* but went on to write that *'The wearing anxiety about the war is not at your dear boy's end of the journey, but with father and mother at home'*. Our mother believed that the marked reserve that we all felt to be characteristic of him was a legacy of his war experience, which often returned to him in nightmares. To us boys he always seemed very much as John Brunner described his own father, who had migrated from Switzerland to Liverpool in 1832: 'the gentlest of men, never willing to believe evil of others, always ready to impute to them good motives'.

Anne Dyer and I start this brief life of my father with an overview of the vital contribution which my family's firm contributed towards the war effort and end it with a summary of my father's later life but the heart of the book is the story of his service in the First World War. Anne has made a study of Felix's letters from the front, the military context of his service and the support he received from family and friends. My family is grateful to her. And I am delighted to publish her story, which, giving pride of place to the letters themselves, she tells so well.

Hugo Brunner
2021

THE BRUNNER FAMILY AND
THE GREAT WAR

MY father's letters were addressed to a family that was much engaged in the war. Throughout the conflict his father was the Member of Parliament for Northwich, as well as an executive director of the family business which played a significant part in the war effort. That was attested to in January 1919 when the director-general of the Explosives Department of David Lloyd George's Ministry of Munitions, Lord Moulton, wrote to my great uncle Roscoe, the chairman of Brunner Mond. His letter included the words *'We are indebted to your company for the manufacture of the bulk of the largest component of the high explosives used by this country in the war'.*[1]

When war broke out in August 1914, the chemical business established by my great grandfather, John Tomlinson Brunner, and Ludwig Mond had been manufacturing pure alkali (soda ash) in their works at Winnington near Northwich, Cheshire for forty years.

1. Sir John Tomlinson Brunner 1842-1919, MP, Pro-Chancellor of the University of Liverpool 1909-1918, by Arthur Hacker.

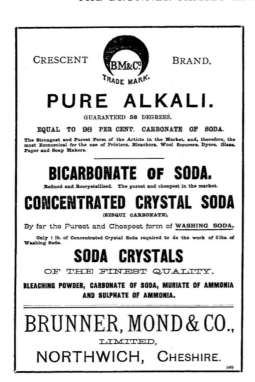

2. Brunner Mond advertisement circa 1891.

John Brunner had been born in Everton, Liverpool in 1842 to a Swiss father and a Manx mother. Mond arrived in England, a trained scientist, from Cassel in Germany aged 22 in 1862. They met at the soda works of John Hutchinson in Widnes, where Brunner was office manager. They got on well. Ten years later, on the basis of a licence to manufacture soda ash by the ammonia-soda process developed by the Solvay family in Belgium, they set up in business together. The Solvay process was more efficient and cleaner than the Leblanc process used by the established manufacturers. So the company prospered.

And in 1914 it was sitting pretty as the largest maker of sodium carbonate for, according to one of its advertisements, *'the use of printers, bleachers, wool scourers, dyers, glass, paper and soap makers'*. *'In the first few months of the war'*, as WJ Reader, the historian of ICI, was to put it, *'there seemed no reason why [the company] should be very directly affected by any demand arising from it. They would go on making soda ash for the industries that needed it'*. [2]

That stance would have suited John Brunner very well in some ways. Once his business had begun to flourish, he had turned his attention to the needs of the communities in which his employees lived. In 1885 he entered Parliament as Liberal MP for the Northwich constituency. He remained an MP until 1909, was appointed a baronet in 1895 and a Privy Councillor in 1906. These facts make him seem a conventional politician, but his biographer, Stephen Koss, chose the sub-title of his biography of my great-grandfather, *Radical Plutocrat*, accurately. Yes, he proclaimed his new-found wealth by personally funding three schools, a free library, a village hall and two guildhalls in his area. But he also expressed his radicalism in active support for home rule in Ireland, Church disestablishment, land reform, welfare legislation (including the terms on which his workers were employed), naval disarmament and the international peace movement. He vigorously opposed the competitive build-up of armaments among the nations of Europe. As late as November 1913, he was declaring to the National Liberal Federation, of which he was the president *'I hate this gross, growing mad expenditure. ... I warn you to resist the secret international organisation of the makers of war material. ... I warn you that the daily Press will be suborned and induced to publish statements inciting to international hatred. It is the devil's business'.*[3]

This kind of language got him into trouble, once Britain went to war. During its first winter he was subjected to ferocious attacks in the press, notably from the journalist and fervent patriot, Horatio Bottomley, who made good use of his victim's Germanic name and pre-war advocacy of disarmament. Bottomley inspired others to write hate mail. One such letter, from a Leicester paper merchant, was addressed to *'Those German Swine, Rt. Hon. Sir John Brunner, MP and Sir Alfred Mond, MP'* [Ludwig's younger son]. It read: *'Hope you are satisfied with devastation and misery caused by your fellow hogs in Germany'.*[4] My ancestor successfully sued the paper merchant – and Bottomley – for libel. Bottomley went to prison after the war for floating fraudulent 'Victory' bonds.

But, no thanks to Bottomley, John Brunner supported the war. Years later, in his note of introduction to his letters from the front, my father spoke for the whole family when he wrote, *'The outbreak of war raised no doubts in the family, we all felt horrified by the invasion of Belgium and felt that Germany must be resisted. Our close business association with the Solvay family who were our largest shareholder doubtless added strength to our feelings of outrage'.*[5]

John not only supported the war, he became unexpectedly involved in it. In pursuing an active public life he had not abandoned the chemical industry. In August 1914 he was chairman of Brunner Mond, and his son Roscoe was managing director. At first the company made patriotic noises and encouraged its employees to volunteer for military service while keeping them partially on the payroll, even allowing senior scientists to go to war. These included the chief scientist, Francis Freeth. He came from a military family and was an enthusiastic Territorial Army officer, who to his dying day liked to be addressed as Major rather than Doctor or Professor. Freeth enlisted in August 1914 and early in the new year went to Flanders, only to be whisked

3. John Fletcher Moulton, 1st Baron Moulton.

back to Northwich within days. He had refused to leave until threatened with arrest. For his services in the war Freeth received an OBE and was later elected a Fellow of the Royal Society.

By the autumn of 1914 the short, mobile war expected by the General Staff had turned into trench warfare. The guns would be needed not so much to kill men (shrapnel shells, containing virtually no explosive material, sufficed for that) as to batter fortifications, a task for which high explosives were essential. The resources to do this were woefully inadequate. This was the shell crisis. The government ordnance factories had never undertaken the manufacture of high explosives and commercial businesses only to a small extent. As the true nature of the war revealed itself, Asquith's government acted.

In November 1914 it appointed the 70-year-old John Fletcher Moulton chairman of a Committee for Explosive Services. Lord Moulton was an amazing man. A distinguished scientist (Fellow of the Royal Society for research in electricity and with expertise in chemistry too), he was also a successful patent lawyer, a court of appeal judge and a parliamentarian. Throughout the war he worked ten-hour days and at weekends and took only ten days off work in four years. During this period the production of high explosives rose from 3,500 tons in 1915 to 236,000 tons in 1918. He is little known now but he was surely one of the heroes of the war. The high explosive required by the army for its bursting charge was Trinitrotoluene (TNT). Moulton soon realised that he would not be able to produce enough toluene to fill all the shells that were needed with TNT as their bursting charge. But he believed that he could get an equally powerful explosive by mixing ammonium nitrate with TNT, a compound known as amatol, comprising as much as 80% ammonium nitrate. He had problems as he set about turning belief into reality. The first was that the generals and admirals didn't agree with him and advanced technical arguments against amatol. The second was that he could not deliver enough amatol unless a large-scale process for making it could be devised.

Early on, he was at Brunner Mond's door, for the company had experience of a wide range of chemicals. Also going for it was the fact that *the manufacture of ammonium nitrate had affinities with the production of ammonium chloride and with the ammonia-soda process*.[6] He might have added 'and by an original process which enabled the country to dispense with importing materials from Chile and Norway'. This was the great achievement of Freeth and his team. Sir Peter Allen (chairman of ICI, 1969–72) told the story that one morning Moulton arrived at Freeth's laboratory in Winnington, having been driven by his chauffeur from London overnight. He took Freeth's arm and said, *'My dear Freeth, do you realise the safety of England depends on this?'*, to which Freeth replied *'In that case, Sir, I'll tell you the truth, I'm certain that these processes will all work'.*[7] They did. And with a little help from the Royal Laboratory at Woolwich, Moulton won the battle with the Ordnance Board which gave him the go-ahead in April 1915.

Ammonium Nitrate plants were built at four places in Cheshire, and at Stratton, Swindon. The plants at Plumley, Lostock and Sandbach, all in Cheshire, were Brunner Mond operations. The Victoria Works in Cheshire and the big plant in Wiltshire were designed by the company but built and operated by the War Department on land it had requisitioned. They were among twenty-three such national factories, officially designated His Majesty's Explosives Factories, which were enabled by the terms of the Defence of the Realm Act of November 1914.

In 1915 the company was asked to solve two other major problems in the making of high explosives. The first was how to make synthetic phenol for manufacturing lyddite, a high explosive then still in use by the British and French navies. The technical problem was cracked and manufacturing started up, also in Cheshire, at Ellesmere Port, in July.

The other problem was the purification of TNT. At that time Brunner Mond had a factory close to residential property at Silvertown on the north bank of the Thames opposite Greenwich. It had been idle since 1912. Moulton directed the company to adapt the factory for purifying TNT by recrystallization from a solution in alcohol. They did so against the advice of Freeth, who described the undertaking as *'manifestly very dangerous'*. A much

4. The Venesta factory, which produced wood veneer packing cases for the tea trade, in ruins following the detonation of TNT at the Brunner Mond explosives works in Silvertown, East London in January 1917.

larger Brunner Mond factory at Gadbrook in Cheshire began operations for the same purpose, but using a new process, in February 1916. Gadbrook was staffed mostly by women, part of a female work force in the company that reached nearly 2,500 in January 1918. But Silvertown was kept on because purified TNT was so desperately needed. The Cheshire plant had experienced several fires but worse befell Silvertown. On the evening of 19 January 1917 fire broke out in the factory and within 6 or 7 minutes it reached the TNT store. Fifty tonnes exploded, killing 73 people, injuring over 400 and causing great damage to property. The explosion could be heard from the Norfolk to the Sussex coasts. Wartime censorship soon exerted its influence over reports of the disaster and there is only passing reference to Silvertown in my father's letters which were themselves subject to censorship.

The Great War changed John Brunner's professional life but it touched his family members too. His two sons spent the war directing the company but two grandsons and three nephews saw action, two of whom were killed. Major Wilfred Brunner of the Royal Engineers was killed at Gallipoli in August 1915 and his younger brother, Godfrey, was wounded there although

*5. Hon Mrs Ethel J Blyth
M.B.E Commandant The
Grange Auxiliary Hospital,
Chertsey 1915-1919.*

he survived the war to end it as a staff officer in Flanders. Captain Cecil
Brunner, a gunner like Felix, died at Passchendaele in October 1917. Felix's
cousin, Sid Buckley MC, served in the Royal Flying Corps and features in
a book *The Escaping Club.* Having been shot down and captured while ob-
serving over German lines, he and its author, A J Evans, spent 17 days on the
run from captivity in Bavaria and reached Switzerland safely in June 1917.
Felix commented on this in a letter to his mother *'Sid's escape is splendid'.*[8]

The ladies of the family also played their part. Two daughters of John
Tomlinson Brunner were awarded MBEs in 1918 for their work as the full
time Commandants of auxiliary hospitals in Braintree, Essex and Chertsey in
Surrey. Maud Gold and Ethel (Effie) Blyth served in this capacity throughout the war. Their cousin, Beatrice Brunner, left her stage career to work first
as a 'canteener' and later as a nurse in Flanders for the French Red Cross.
She was awarded the Croix de Guerre for her service. Felix's sister Joyce also
worked as a nurse in various auxiliary hospitals in Cheshire.

The youngest member of the family to go to war was my father. In the
course of his duties as an artillery officer he was of course responsible for the
accurate firing of shells which will have contained explosives manufactured
by his family's firm.

FELIX BRUNNER'S WAR

F ELIX Brunner was a very young man when he went to war in April
1917. After a short period of training in Ireland and on Salisbury Plain,
he was commissioned and posted to the Ypres Salient[1], where he first
experienced combat and its consequences. Felix was then posted to an Intelligence gathering role, which was not without high risk, but went back
into combat for the final months of the war as the Allied armies advanced
through Belgium into Germany.

Between September 1916 and December 1918 he wrote over 300 letters
to his family which chronicle in vivid detail some of the disturbing events he
witnessed but also allow us insights into the personality and daily life of this
young officer on the battlefields of Flanders.

Training and combat September 1916 – July 1917

In the Spring of 1916, Felix was interviewed by the Royal Artillery training
branch at St John's Wood barracks in London, having left Cheltenham College the previous year. After a term at Trinity College, Oxford, he reported

1. *Felix (middle row, third from right) aged 17 pictured with his house rugby team.*

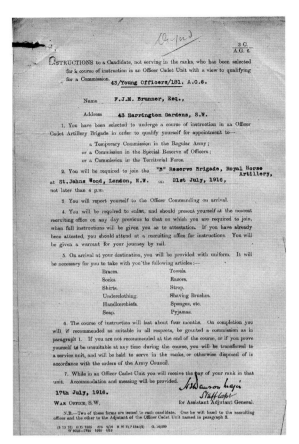

2. Instructions to report to St John's Wood barracks. Extract from Felix Brunner's Service Record.

to the Cadet barracks there in July. There followed a period of six months in which he received training in gunnery and equestrianism (horses provided the power to move guns into position and their care and training was fundamental to operational effectiveness). Other skills were acquired such as semaphore and morse code signalling. Felix was posted to Salisbury Plain for a short course firing live shells where he noted that the trainees were not allowed ear protection which *'was distinctly trying on the ears.'* [2]

Felix was commissioned as 'Second Lieutenant, Special Reserve of Officers' in November. [3] He was posted to Brighton Barracks where he met the son of Herbert Asquith who seemed *'a nice fellow quite easy going & without much push & go.'* [4]

Further training in Ireland in January[5] and February 1917 included a course which exposed him to tear gas in order to encourage the nimble application of a gas mask: *'Every man is gassed before going abroad... they let loose the asphyxiating gas which made no impression on the helmets I am glad to say.'* [6]

Felix went on leave in March before he embarked to join the war in

France. It was probably then that Sir Luke Fildes painted the portrait of the young 2nd Lieutenant which now hangs at Greys Court in Oxfordshire. [7]

In early April 1917 Felix sailed from Southampton to Le Havre. The voyage was unpleasant as it was cold and windy on deck and *'hopelessly thick down below where all the port holes were closed.'* The boat then anchored in open sea for a while *'with disastrous effect'*.[8] Once in France at the base depot, Felix found that spring snow lay on the ground, as it had in southern England before he left. A long time later, a fellow subaltern reminded him of that cold spring:

> *'We shared a small hut together and slept on the floor in our sleeping bags. One morning when I awoke I found that I could not move my head, for during the night the moisture of my breath had frozen my chin to the blankets. You saved the situation by chipping away the ice and setting my head free.'* [9]

Felix was assigned to the censoring of letters and found it monotonous but occasionally amusing: *'One gentleman said about a photo of his lady friend 'you look quite a picture not altered at all in fact you look fatter'.'* [10] During this time Felix enjoyed a concert in the sergeant's mess by gunners and drivers *'all 'artistes' in civil life'* [11] which was very good fun, he felt, but that day he was also posted to the 'right' division, the 25th division of the 2nd British Army. On the 7th April he left for the front with 2 NCOs and 35 men and remarked on the peacefulness of the countryside only 6 to 8 miles from the front line.[12] Three days later the War Diary of 112th battery, Royal Field Ar-

Place	Date	Hour	Summary of Events and Information	Remarks and references to Appendices
In The Field.	April 1st. 1917.		General Duties and fatigues at Wagon Lines - One Officer and 20 men per battery still working at STEENWERCK.	
-do-	2nd.		General duties and fatigues at Wagon Lines - One Officer and 20 men per battery still working at STEENWERCK.	
	3rd.		Colonel and Battery commanders went over to NEUVE EGLISE to arrange details of relief of 1st N.Z.F.A. Bde.	
	4th.		Adjutant and Signals Officers preceeded to H.Q. 1st N.Z.F.A. Bde. One section of each Battery relieved one section of each Battery of the 1st N.Z.F.A. Bde. All exchanged guns except B/112 who had to bring in one section.	
	5th.		Remaining sections completed relief - All guns being exchanged - Command passed to Colonel Forman at 10.p.m. - At 12 midnight A/112 came tactically under the command of O.C. 3rd N.Z.F.A. Bde, and we covered 1 Battalion front (From U.15.a.1.2. to W-E Road with B, C, and D Batteries.)	
	6th.		Enemy shelled T.15.d. with about 250 - 4.2" and 5.9" between 8.a.m. and 9.30.a.m.	
	7th		About 7.p.m. airfight between 8 of our machines and about 10 German scouts. One of our machines landed in our lines with observer killed and pilot wounded, another crashed in flames in our lines.	
	8th		Work still continuing on gun positions - About 200 rounds 5.9" (a few being gas) fired into N.32, 33, and T.2.	
	9th		Great VIMY offensive starts.	
	10th		2nd Lieut. BRUNNER J.M. joined the Brigade and was posted to "A" Battery - Weather very bad and snowy.	

3. *Excerpt from the war diary of 112th Brigade Royal Field Artillery recording Felix Brunner's arrival.*

tillery, reported that

> *'2nd Lieut. BRUNNER [F] J. M. joined the Brigade and was posted to 'A'
> Battery – Weather very bad and snowy.'* [13]

Felix was nineteen years old and among the officers commanding one of
three sections in the battery, responsible for two 18 pounder guns and wag-
ons pulled by six-horse teams.

The following day Felix went to the front. His battery was positioned behind Hill 63, about seven miles south of Ypres, near Neuve Eglise, looking
towards Warneton and the German lines in front of Messines Ridge.

Felix described his first day at the gun lines in a letter to his father written later that afternoon. [14] He travelled from a comfortable and safe billet and
after two lorry journeys and a walk passed through a practically deserted
village to the battery position. Along with the battery commander, Major
Duncan Campbell, and a Captain Fraser,

> *'We started out & went at a most furious pace up the hill which was very
> muddy & covered with shell holes. After a bit the major drew his revolver &
> proceeded to advance cautiously…on enquiring from the captain [I] learned that
> it was not Fritz but a partridge he was stalking.'*

They arrived at the dugout and the Lieutenant on duty pointed out the spot
on the horizon which marked the zero line of the battery's zone. (The zero
line was an imaginary line, expressed as a compass bearing, running up the
centre of the projected area of fire.)

> *'Then [he] said 'I'll just show you' & (to the telephonist) 'Number 3 gun ac-
> tion' etc. Soon a shell burst right by the spot he had pointed out.'*

Felix experienced being under bombardment for the first time shortly
after and told his father that *'the O.P. [Observation Post] was shelled hard for
a short time with whizz bangs. They dropped all around and it was not very pleas-
ant while it lasted.'* [15] There was virtually no warning of this type of incoming
shell, because the shell travelled faster than the speed of sound and the noise
of the gun firing was heard after the shell was fired. The whizz bangs were
consequently much feared.

Felix himself commanded a bombardment on the 21st April [16] and made
his first visit to the infantry on the front line. This was the first time he saw
a fatality. He was told that a man had been killed a short while before he arrived and that retaliation was deemed appropriate. Felix found a telephone
dugout and rang through only to find that firing had already been ordered.
He emerged to find *'two men removing the remains of the poor fellow… I returned
rather subdued.'* [17]

Felix acted as liaison officer between the artillery and the infantry and in

4. Royal Field Artillery 18 pounder battery preparing to open fire near Meteren 13 April 1918.

early May he was appointed a section commander with 52 men, 50 horses, 2 guns and 10 other vehicles under his authority.[18] In letters to his parents Felix details gas attacks, the lack of sleep and the constant daily shelling by both armies, so much so that two guns were out of action because the bore was worn down.[19] He admits to being

> *'rather impressed with the scene here at night. The whole country is flickering with gun flashes, and Very lights are continually rising and falling. You can hear the pop-pop-pop…of machine guns more or less continuously. They are always more active by night than by day. Roads, in full view of the Hun, deserted by day, are crowded with horses and mule transport bringing up ammunition and supplies to the batteries and the trenches.'* [20]

Throughout April and into May Felix continued the light hearted tone apparent in his earlier letters whilst training, such as on 28 April when he writes to his father that

> *'The shells were whizzing over my head at a tremendous rate and bursting beautifully on the Boche Line'*

or on 13 May, writing again to his father, that after a bathhouse he was intending to use received a direct hit from German shells he returned to his battery and, irritated, gave *'Boche a liberal quantity of 'iron rations''*. In the same letter he noted that

> *'Thanks to BM & Co* [the family firm, Brunner Mond] *& the rest we have now got a fine large allotment of stuff to blaze away. This means much better fun for the*

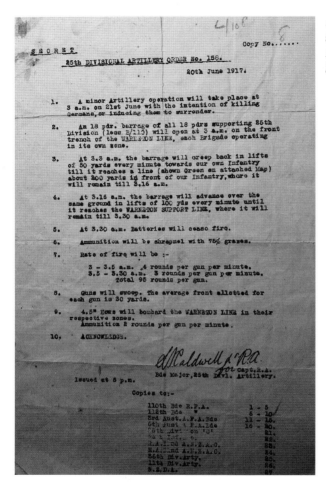

5. Operating Order issued to Felix's battery. Found in a collection of his papers and artefacts.

FOO [Forward Observation Officer] *but also more work both day and night at the battery.'*

A letter of 25 May to his sister related an interaction with a senior officer, *'a very military gentleman, [who] likes prompt & direct replies at all costs…*

COL. *Are those trees down there poplars?*

SELF *I'm not quite sure, Sir, people seem to call them poplars out here, but they are not very like English poplars.*

COL (fiercely) *ARE THEY OR ARE THEY NOT POPLARS?*

SELF *(desperately with complete decision) YES, SIR, THEY ARE*

 (Result absolute satisfaction)'

6. Position of Hill 63 behind Messines Ridge and the changing British front lines as the battle progressed June 7 – June 11, 1917.

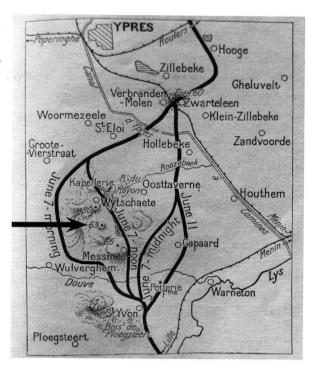

He may well have been attempting to reassure his family in using this tone but was also perhaps yet to appreciate fully the impact of the events in which he was taking part.

Felix's tone became much more sombre in a letter of 8 June 1917 to his father which detailed the action in which he took part the previous day. Throughout 1917 tunnelling under Messines Ridge had been continuing in conditions of great secrecy, the objective being to remove the German Army from its positions on the high ground of the ridge as a prelude to the next phase of the campaign, which included the 3rd battle of Ypres, generally known as the battle of Passchendaele.

Felix was witness to the conclusion of this work when, at 3.05 am on the 7th, 21 mines placed in these tunnels were exploded under the German lines. Within 30 seconds a series of huge explosions created 19 large craters, [21] still visible in the landscape today, and killed around 10,000 German soldiers. The explosions were heard as far away as London and were probably the largest planned explosion in history prior to the first atomic bomb test in 1945. General Herbert Plumer, commander of the British Second Army, told his officers the evening before that while they may not make history, they would certainly change the geography. They did both.

A young artilleryman, Aubrey Wade, described the shock wave as the

7. *German trench on Messines Ridge 7 June 1917.*

mines exploded:

> *The ground under our feet literally rocked. It writhed again as the spreading wave of shock from the annihilated Messines Ridge broke upon us and passed on. A sudden rising wind blew back over the line into our faces, a fearful hot wind like a breath from the Pit itself...Swift on the heels of the wind came a vast, ever-growing roar as the guns opened up all along the line.* [22]

Felix told his father that

> 'At five minutes past three the sky to the East became suddenly red and the Earth shook several times. Mines were exploding. At ten past three the guns opened up and the infantry went over. We put up a shrapnel barrage firing first on the front line and lifting gradually to the top of the Ridge. The barrage lasted 100 minutes. The Ridge was then in our hands. We stopped firing for about half an hour and then opened up a slow rate of fire on targets given us by aeroplanes.'

Felix's battery commander, Major Campbell, along with a signaller Cpl J Mayes, were killed in the battle. Felix movingly recounted his reaction to Major Campbell's death:

> 'It is a very bad blow for us all... He was absolutely one of the best. He worked

8. Above; British soldiers looking into a huge mine crater blown up on the morning of the battle.

9. Right; Spanbroekmolen crater in November 2009, also known as 'Lone Tree Crater' or 'Pool of Peace'. It was created on 7 June 1917 by one of the mines exploded during the battle.

> *harder than any man in the battery and thought of nothing except to give the Infantry the best possible support. He was only thirty-three but looked ten years older...'*

The Brigade's war diary, however, noted that

> *'Attack ... on Messines Ridge was entirely successful. All objectives were gained.'* [23]

Felix recalled in later life that the division to which he was attached remained in action on the ridge for nearly a further fortnight and that they were very exposed to German guns:

> *'The main trouble was the success of our bombardment which destroyed any means of concealment. Every time we fired the guns by day great clouds of dust hung in the air advertising our presence to observers in enemy balloons. So we were really pinned down and shot at by much heavier guns with dire results.'* [24]

The German army, overwhelmed on Messines Ridge, utilised huge naval guns positioned miles outside the British range. Felix's friend, Gilbert Laithwaite, reported in a letter to the president of Trinity College that Felix had *'two thrilling escapes from Boche retaliation on his battery'* [25] at this time. Felix reported briefly on some of the officers who became casualties,

```
B.E.F.
    8/6/17                                                    Friday
```

Dear Father,

Since I last wrote I have been taking a very small part in a big
and I think very successful fight as far as it has gone so far. Both
ourselves and the Huns had been expecting it for a long time. The
German communiqués nearly every day for the last fortnight had reported
increasing artillery activity. A recent one had it that the bombardment
had reached 'an intense violence'. None of us knew the day of the attack
('Zero' day) until the afternoon before. At about 8pm on Wednesday when
we were at dinner the hour of attack (Zero hour) came through. I am not
giving away any secrets when I tell you that the time was 3.10 A.M.

(Sat. aft. cont. 6 P.M.) I have found no time to continue this letter
until now.

         I went to bed at 10.30 P.M. & arranged to be called at 2.15.
At 3 we were standing by ready to fire. The Boche had been putting over
tear gas a short time before & it was maddeningly irritating for a short
time. At five minutes past three the sky to the east became suddenly
red and the earth shook several times. Mines were exploding. At ten
past three the guns opened up and the infantry went over. We put up a
shrapnel barrage firing first on the front line and lifting gradually to
the top of the Ridge. The barrage lasted 100 minutes. The Ridge was
then in our hands. We stopped firing for about half an hour and opened
up a slow rate of fire on targets given us by aeroplanes. At 7 the Major
went forward to reconnoitre with the Sergt. Major, his orderly and some
signallers.

         Soon afterwards Dean followed with a party to prepare a road
for the guns to advance over No Man's Land to a position which it was
intended to take up in the Boche lines. Capt. Fraser, Radford and myself
waited for orders to move as soon as the road was passable. During the
morning we had orders from Division not to attempt to cross the former
No Man's Land as the Huns were firing heavily on the part we were to
cross and on the position in which we had intended to come into action.
We were told to take up position further back with the other batteries
of our group. Capt. Fraser sent me on to find out the way. That was
easy enough. When I came to the position the wounded were streaming
back. Sometimes you would see an Englishman leaning on a German or some
unwounded German prisoners carrying one of their own fellows. I returned
to the Battery and we all came along. Just as we were about to get into
action we had orders to wait until Major Campbell should send back a
report as to the chances of our getting into the forward position after

all. We waited several hours, and then as we heard nothing from the Major, the Colonel told us to get into action just in front of where we were waiting. While they were getting the guns into position I worked out a line of fire as well as I could with a map blowing about in the wind & a protractor (that I had just received the night before). We were soon firing.

The Sergt. Major returned late in the evening in rather shaky condition. The Major's party had reconnoitred the Battery position and then went forward to find an O.P. on the Ridge. When at the O.P. the orderly got hit above the knee and the Major came down with him as far as where Dean's party was working and then returned up the ridge where he had left the S-M and a signaller. He was very shaken when Dean saw him and when he left with the Corporal Signaller he remarked 'It's either a grave or Blighty for me'. The S-M stayed on top of the Ridge until about 5.30 and then came back having seen nothing of either the Major or the Corporal. On Friday morning the S-M went to look for them and found both killed no doubt instantaneously. A party fetched them in later in the day and they were buried in a cemetery near here this morning. It is a very bad blow for us all though of course not so much for me as for those who have been with him since the Division was formed in England. He was absolutely one of the best. He worked harder than any man in the battery and thought nothing except to give the Infantry the best possible support. He was only thirty three but looked ten years older as he was already rather bald above the forehead. He was the biggest man in the battery, not less than 6 ft 1 I should think.

We have been living in rough and ready style since we came here. We couldn't bring up our kits except just a little bedding. I brought up my air mattress which has proved a tremendous comfort as we have had nothing softer than wooden 'duckboards' to lie on the last two nights. I recommend it most strongly. We have found a dugout but unfortunately it is about 30 yds in front of the guns. We can't light a candle in it when they are firing as the concussion blows it out! I had only one gun in my section during the barrage. It came from ordnance later on Tuesday when we had moved forward and most kindly brought up with it a parcel from Fortnum & Mason's and two letters!

I must close this long letter now. I hope you get it before very long. I am very fit I am glad to say.

Your loving son

Felix Brunner

10. Transcript of Felix Brunner's letter to his father, John, describing the action he witnessed during the battle of Messines Ridge 7 June 1917.

'There seemed no need to pile on the agony by describing the misfortunes of the other ranks. We tied up the wounded and despatched them to the rear with varying degrees of hopefulness as to their chance of survival.' [26]

Over the following month Felix experienced more of the harsh realities of life and death on the front line. A fellow subaltern was shot in the back whilst only a few yards from Felix during a reconnaissance mission for the Brigade. He told his father that he was on his way to an Observation Post with another officer and that:

'When we were about 60 yards away some bullets came very near. Fraser... said 'I'm hit' & fell into a shell hole. I was about 5 yds. away and instinctively did the same thing. I crawled along to him & was relieved to find that he was not bad...So we crawled back very flat to the O.P.' [27]

In late June Felix took his battery to the wagon lines for a few days where they and the horses could rest, and bathe, and maintenance was performed.[28]

Early the following month a shell burst over Felix's gun while it was firing, wounded three of his men, and as more shells came over one burst in front of the dugout where Felix would have been sleeping, injuring another subaltern.[29] While Felix did not keep these events from his family nevertheless he did not tell them exactly how very heavy the fighting was or just how many casualties, both men and horses, were being inflicted.

On 6 July Felix was posted to 29th division with General Edward Hall Stevenson as his commanding officer, who was married to his mother's first cousin. He remarked to his father in a letter on that date that he had experienced three months active service and had got to know all the men, the veterans amongst whom believed the battle they had just experienced to be worse than the Somme.

Intelligence and Reconnaissance officer July 1917 – July 1918

Felix's role was to collect together reports, aerial photographs and maps about the German occupied area ahead of the front line and to provide analysis and summary, including hand drawn 'panoramas', of all appropriate information for the Field Artillery. His function also became that of Reconnaissance Officer after his predecessor in that position was killed by a sniper. [30] He had to be familiar with the position of the front line and that of the German forces facing it and often he was required to perform reconnaissance to do so which could be very dangerous.

The day after his arrival at Divisional HQ Felix accompanied a General on a tour of the front line (in a Sunbeam car) at 3.15 in the morning. He wryly remarked that it was the safest time for Generals to do such work.[31] He specifically told his mother on 11 July that he could not tell her much

11. A photographic panorama of the front line found in Felix's papers.

about his role but on 16th of that month told his father that he was very busy compiling and delivering six reports a day and that he had to go up to the Observation Posts to do so, which was very dangerous, and he had to sprint very low between them. Felix described his attitude to shell-fire to his sister Joyce on 26th July, telling her that at first it seemed exciting but that now it seemed futile:

> 'The real great wonder of the war is that anyone has stuck to it for so long'.

He told his father on 25 July that his job was to summarise reports which came in from the brigades every morning and circularise them. The great advantage of this staff role was that he got regular sleep, except when on night

12. A Royal Artillery Observation Officer signalling the results of firing back to the battery.

duty. He told his mother that on 29 July he was woken at 1am to be told of a gas attack by *'a gentleman whose identity was hidden by a gas mask…I confirmed this information with a few sniffs…It was most annoying'*. Gas shells made an ominous *'whizz-phut'* sound and landed with a thud but no bang so that it was easy to imagine that they were *'duds'*. [32] The gas soon dispersed, and he went back to sleep.

Notwithstanding Felix's airy tone in describing such events, danger was always present. The next month Felix was sitting next to the driver in a car while on reconnaissance when the driver was shot in the knee. [33] The following month he describes seeing

> *'a general, 3 subalterns and sundry 'other ranks' in the attitude adopted by Mohammedans at prayer* [due to] *a very efficient 5.9in shell which thought fit to burst just in front of the battery.'* [34]

In October, whilst moving forward to observe the German front line, Felix was strafed by a German plane and had to shelter in a 'smelly' pill box, listening to the bullets hit the concrete. [35] Felix noted that he had heard of the death of his friend Joscelyne, with whom he went up to Oxford, but had not written to Joscelyne's parents as he knew so many who had been killed that he didn't think about writing unless he had served directly with them. [36]

During this time, between July and December 1917, the battle of Passchendaele was in progress. Felix was not on the front line but as a reconnaissance officer was always close and frequently visited it. He later told his mother: *'To have missed the worst part of all that appalling battle in Flanders is no small thing.'* [37]

Felix was witness to the opening barrage of the Battle of Cambrai in November 1917 and watched the first large scale use of tanks in a military offensive:

> *'Suddenly at twenty past six all the batteries hidden in all kinds of places opened up with an almost simultaneous roar and flash and the tanks moved forward.'* [38]

Felix went across No Man's Land into the German lines and reported that many prisoners of war were taken.

The battle was closely followed by a huge German counter attack whilst Felix was at HQ at Gouzeaucourt, south west of Cambrai. During the attack General Stevenson, his commanding officer, was wounded after a shell burst near to him and he was hit just below the knee. Almost immediately after he had been attended to by a doctor:

> *'…there was a great rattle of rifle and machine gun fire and it seemed that the Boches must have broken through…In a very few minutes the Huns came over*

13. Tank 'Hilda' of H battalion led a 6 mile line of 350 tanks at the battle of Cambrai.

the hill less than a hundred yards away and began shooting right down on us with machine guns and rifles. We had about a hundred yards to go along a road then to crawl under a train drawn across the road and then another four or five hundred yards of road to cross before we could get any cover. Of course they fired hard at us all the way along.' [39]

Such was the speed of the German advance that Felix and his fellow officer were ordered to leave Stevenson behind. Felix remained within a few hundred yards of where Stevenson lay for the rest of the day but could not get near enough to him to pull him to safety. The next day an infantry counter attack managed to rescue Stevenson but his injury was serious enough to end his war. The same counter attack recovered a few items of equipment which Felix had abandoned including the paper on which he wrote a letter to his mother the following day, although he kept Stevenson's 'muffler', which he felt was of no immediate use to the General.

Felix had an extended period of leave over mid-December 1917 into January 1918 due to heavy snowfall, which meant that he could not return to duty on time, but had done so by 9 January. He continued with his reconnaissance duties and told his mother that the area was *'very quiet but the country was the most appalling wilderness I had ever seen, nothing but mud and water-logged shell-holes as far as one can see.'* [40]

B.E.F.
            1/12/17

    I am writing to explain the rather cryptic wire that was sent to
you today, as far as is possible, without running my head up against the
Censor.

    First you need not worry about Hall in the least. I am quite sure
he will be all right now though he must have had a very trying twenty
four hours or so after he was hit. He was just on his way from the dugout
where he slept to the one where we had our mess when a shell burst near
and hit him just below the knee and one of the servants in the same
place. We got him into a deep tunnelled dugout and a doctor tied him up.
It was apparently only a flesh wound and the bone was not broken. Almost
immediately after this there was a great rattle of rifle and machine gun
fire and it seemed that the Boches must have broken through. It grew
louder every minute and things looked rather black especially as we
were practically unarmed except for a few revolvers. Tommy rather wanted
myself or him to stay with Hall as it seemed such a horribly low trick to
run away and leave him alone wounded. He asked one of the G.S.O's. what
he should do and the reply was that it was no good staying as it would
only mean getting captured and as he or I was unwounded and Hall could
not walk we should not be able to stay together. In a very few minutes
the Huns came over the hill less than a hundred yards away and began
shooting right down on us with machine guns and rifles. We had about a
hundred yards to go along a road then to crawl under a train drawn across
the road and then another four or five hundred yards of road to cross
before we could get any cover. Of course they fired hard at us all the
way along. By an absolute marvel Tommy, [*the Brigade Major*] Cunnison [*a
staff captain*] myself and some others got through safely, I can't say very
much more but the Boche didn't get much further on. I remained for the
rest of the day within a few hundred yards of where Hall was, hoping to
get back to see whether he was still there. As we didn't manage to push
the Huns back quite far enough, I left to find the others just before it
became dark. Next morning the infantry attacked and got farther enough on
to get Hall out. We had almost given up hope of finding him there so you
may imagine how delighted we were to hear he was safe in hospital. I went
there to see him but he had just left. Of course we have lost practically
all our kit. There is just a chance that we may recover a little so I
am waiting till we find out before I send any requests to 43. [*Harrington
Gardens — Felix's family home*] We have borrowed some blankets and things
so are only rather uncomfortable. Some parcels for Hall arrived this
afternoon. One was a muffler and I felt sure that as Hall had no immediate
use for it you would not mind my keeping it as every little helps. Please
show this letter to 43 as I have no more time to write now.
                Your affect.nephew,
                    Felix Brunner

15. The former battlefield of Passchendaele near Broodseinde, 11 January 1918.

The prospect, or lack of prospect, of 'Blighty' or home leave being granted is a frequent theme in Felix's letters.[41] British army officers were supposed to have home leave every three months, in theory, the rank and file every fifteen months on average.[42] The period of leave referred to above, in December 1917 and January 1918, was mentioned in a letter to Felix's sister in July of 1918 in which he writes that this was the last time he had a home leave.[43] A letter of October 1918 refers to the minimum time between leave for officers as being five months.[44] Felix appears to have had five periods of home leave in the time covered by his letters between September 1916 and December 1918. [45]

The availability of leave depended on a number of different circumstances ranging from the lack of officers available to a particular section, due to casualty rates or illness (flu was present amongst Felix's comrades during 1918 and Felix himself had flu in June),[46] the imminence of combat, or simply it not being one's turn. Officers were allowed leave more locally, and Felix refers to shopping in the local town, or 'Paris leave'.[47] He relates a rather bitter song he heard when attending an entertainment to celebrate his birthday in October of 1917:

14. Opposite; Transcript of Felix Brunner's letter to General Stevenson's wife describing the action in which her husband was injured.

'If you live to be ninety-four
And stick it out till the end of the war
You may get leave but not before
In these hard times' [48]

Felix tells of his friend

'Tarrant who is still rather embittered at having been turned back just as he was
starting on leave' [49] and reckoned that *'I think I should have been soured for*
life at least' [50] if that had happened to him.

The prospect of home leave was of course crucial for morale as it was a more
realistic short term expectation than the prospect of peace for many at the
front, but Felix was obliged on occasion to tell his family that the prospect
of leave was distant [51] although he tried to keep up their hopes (and perhaps
his own). In August 1918 he told his sister that he had seen a generous leave
allocation which was very cheering as he had not thought he would see her
until the following January *'an idea which even my healthy optimism could not*
quite contemplate with a smile'.

The period between the beginning of 1918 and when Felix returned to
active duty in August was a busy and worrying time as the German Spring
Offensive launched in March quickly took ground which had already been
heavily fought over. Felix mentioned aspects of his work in the letters in-
terspersed with comments which indicated his concern at the progress of
the fighting. He commented lightly on his work to his mother when he described visiting an Observation Post by wading knee deep through trenches
and then crawling: *'It was a lovely afternoon and the Hun were extraordinarily*
amicable.' [52]

In February 1918 Felix wrote to his sister that he

'saw Mr Winston Churchill today... The versatile author-politician-statesman-
soldier-artist was dressed in a Homburg hat, a pair of field boots & a few other
things.' [53]

In June Felix also met the Commander in Chief, Field Marshal Sir Douglas Haig:

'Duggie looked very much like his photos. Rather short, strong jaws etc. He
didn't look very blooming, I thought, which is not perhaps to be wondered at
considering his responsibilities.' [54]

He met some friends and their rough haired terriers, one of whom they had
nursed back to health after it had been gassed the previous autumn. [55] Felix
told his father that he had got out of bed at 2am to go to an Observation Post

16. Winston Churchill as Minister of Munitions, watching the official Allied entry into Lille in October 1918.

17. General Sir Herbert Plumer, Commander of the Second Army, General Sir Herbert Lawrence, Chief of General Staff, Field Marshal Sir Douglas Haig (l-r) on the steps of General HQ Western Front at Montreuil sur Mer, 1918.

by Balloon—Durch Luftballon.

HEUTE SIND SIE DARAN—MORGEN KOMME ICH!

DER TODESRACHEN.

18. British propaganda leaflet collected by Felix. It reads 'The Jaws of Death. Today it's your turn – tomorrow will be mine!'

from where he wanted to draw a panorama of the line and that

> *'It is not my favourite pastime walking about near the front line at night where there are no trenches. The Boche knows of course where the tracks are and puts short and rapid bursts of machine gun fire on them at uncertain intervals.'* [56]

He told his mother that *'We have been pretty busy just lately and it would be absurd to pretend that it is not a serious and anxious time.'* [57] He told her of an experience recounted by his friend Maurice [58] who advised him not to use the attic of a large chateau in sight of the Germans as an Observation Post: '*I was in one today and the first floor welcomed a 4.2… The effect on my morale was regrettable.'* [59]

Later that month he told his father that the loss of Kemmel with *'its marvellous view* [would be] *of the greatest importance'* [60] and worse than a withdrawal from Ypres should it take place.

Felix however was unimpressed by an example of Allied propaganda directed at German troops. Printed in April 1918, this example of a *'Balloon Pamphlet'* was timed to further demoralise German soldiers, already in low spirits after the failure of the Spring Offensive earlier that year. The gentlemen whipping the soldiers into the jaws of death are depicted as financiers and producers of the munitions from which they will profit. The message may have been aimed at stirring discontent amongst the numbers of German troops who had been shipped back from the Eastern Front and had been exposed to the ideas of the Russian revolutionaries.

Felix described Allied planes mistakenly shooting down balloons containing leaflets and sent one to his father. Its crude attempt to influence attitudes and actions *'seems to me a fairly contemptible method of making war!'* [61]

The final months August 1918 – December 1918

In May Felix had been promoted to Lieutenant and in August, as he had requested, he was posted back to active duty with 460th battery, a howitzer battery of the 15th Brigade, Royal Horse Artillery. He informed his father that the first few days were spent being instructed in the use of howitzers, as firing was more complicated than for 18 pounders which he was used to firing, due to the use of varying quantities of propellant with the howitzer instead of a fixed charge with the 18 pounders.[62] Felix told his mother that he was

> *'beginning to earn my pay now… This morning I spent some hours with a working party and shifted quite a lot of shells myself – hard work as each one weighs 35lbs… Sometimes one is ordered to get 2 or 3 thousand rounds into some position in about 2 nights… an immense amount of work… for men and horses.'* [63]

Felix described his work to his sister, telling her of an Observation Post he had been watching for a signal flag of a particular colour, by which the

19. Howitzer firing during the battle of Messines Ridge.

43

20. *A German helmet, stick grenade, range finder and a bayonet in its scabbard recovered by Felix from the battlefields.*

infantry called for artillery support. After lunch he crawled amongst the corn *in front of the trench* (my italics) to find a good view point, coming across the usual things such as boxes of bombs, rifles and helmets of both nationalities, petrol tins (used for water), a dead German soldier, a cross marking another dead soldier and miles of tangled telephone wire. [64]

SECRET. APPENDIX A.
To
15th Brigade R.H.A. OPERATION ORDER No 38.

F.O.Os and COMMUNICATIONS.

1.	The O.C. "B" Battery R.H.A. will detail an officer and necessary signallers to man an O.P. at .
As soon after zero as the visibility is good.

2.	Lieut. F.M. Brunner R.F.A. (460th Battery R.F.A.) will act as F.O.O. to follow up the attack of the 87th Inf. Brigade.
The following party and equipment will report to him at 12 noon on I day.

	Headquarters .... One Telephone.
	"B", "L" and War. Btys. One signaller each.
	460th Battery R.F.A. Five Signallers and one telephone.

3.	He will commence laying a line from R B cable head I 16 a 4 9 and will proceed via YEOMANRY POST I 17 d 5 o to STIRLING CASTLE. The only means of communication will be by telephone.

26.9.18.	Captain, R.H.A.
	Adjutant, 15th Brigade R.H.A.

21. Extract from the war diary of 15th Brigade, Royal Horse Artillery, describing Felix Brunner's orders as Forward Operating Officer in an attempt to lay lines of communication.

It was whilst undertaking a similar operation in September of 1918 that Felix experienced what probably seemed a comparatively mundane series of events at the time but which became the subject of one episode of a television documentary series *The Trench Detectives* called *The Secret Trench*,[65] subsequent to an archaeological dig.

Felix described the event in a letter to his father of 29 September 1918[66] and an Appendix to the Operation Order marked *'Secret'* briefly laid out the actions required of Felix. As Forward Observation Officer (FOO) he was to lay a telephone wire following on from an infantry advance so as to be able to communicate back from the front line and guide artillery targeting. Felix explained to his father that it was arranged for his party to meet one from another brigade at a point on the front line to which a cable had already been laid. The two parties together were to carry sufficient cable to reach the objective. The other party did not turn up in time and Felix and his signaller had to follow on behind the third wave of infantry in the hope that they would follow. He laid all the wire he carried but had to leave a man with the phone at one end and go forward with a signaller, hoping to send news back by this means. It started to rain, however, and the weather became so misty that this proved impossible. Two and half hours later the

```
B.E.F.                                                          29/9/18


Dear Father,
I was entirely unable to write yesterday as I should have done owing I
think I may say now that there is so much fighting going on, to our being
engaged in a big attack. I had the job of F.O.O. [Forward Observation
Officer] for the Bde, my task being to follow up close behind the infantry
laying a wire so as to be able to send back the latest news by telephone.
It was arranged for me to meet a party from the other Bde at a point in
the front line to which a cable had already been laid. The two parties
were to carry sufficient wire to reach our objective. Unfortunately the
other party did not turn up in time so I went over just behind the third
wave of infantry hoping that the others would follow soon. I laid out all
my wire without much difficulty though the shelling was rather unpleasant
at the start. I left a man with a 'phone at the end of the wire and moved
along with a signaller with a flag hoping to send some news back by flag
wagging. Then it began to rain and got so misty that this was impossible
so I just went on to our objective which we took very easily and waited.
After 2 hours the other people turned up with their wire but by that time
it was too late to send back any information worth having.
        As it was the show was a complete success & all went well but it
was a great disappointment to me as one likes to be of some use after
undertaking this not very pleasant sort of job. One gets a lot of kudos
if one is successful in this kind of show. However the battle was a
howling success which was the main thing.
        I hope this letter will reach you in fairly good time. Of course
postal arrangements are a little disorganised at present.

                        Your loving son
                            Felix Brunner
```

22. *Transcript of Felix Brunner's letter to his father describing the actions of 28 September 1918.*

second party turned up, but it was by then too late to send back any useful information. The battle was a success but Felix was disappointed that his role had not proved more useful.

In digging on the site of a trench, which was not marked on contemporary trench maps, archaeologists found a handkerchief as well as a great coat, a water bottle (still containing water) and the remains of a 'flag-wagger', a device made of black and white squares which were pulled up by bamboo rods to reveal the contrasting colour and communicated by Morse Code. Perhaps Felix's signaller had dropped this device when it became useless to their mission. The documentary team traced Felix's name through the brigade war diary. [67]

Around this time the British Army started the series of rapid offensives through France and Belgium into Germany (known as the battle of the Hundred Days) which presaged the end of the war. Felix was obliged to tell his family that they would only hear sporadically from him as the postal service struggled to maintain the extraordinarily efficient service it had previously provided: *'the postal arrangements have entirely gone phut at the moment.'*[68] Roads and railways were repaired at great speed as the old battlefields were left behind and Felix felt that it was

> *'pretty well assured now that the war will be over by this time next year at any rate and very possibly a good deal sooner.'* [69]

Throughout October 1918 Felix only had time to scribble hurried notes and told his father on 18th that he had received a lot of letters but could not reply at present due to the *'strenuous nature of war.'* This letter described the previous night during which he experienced enemy aerial bombing as well as shelling and a machine gun and gas attack. He later described leading his battery to a rendezvous shortly before dark:

> *'As the night was pitchy and I did not know the country I was extremely relieved to arrive at the point selected. It is rather a trying responsibility being in charge of a long column at night and when the roads are blocked by traffic and under shell fire. It is the worst experience that falls to the lot of the gunner…We got the guns into action, unloaded the ammunition and sent the wagon for more.'*

He then reported that

> *'We turned in soon after 1.30 this morning and rose again at about 6.30 AM. We then got an order for the battle which was duly fought at 9 AM after a fearful rush in working out the barrage orders. Before the said barrage was over we had orders that we were not to take part in the advance but to retire this evening whence we came..'*

At this stage he had not had a change of clothes for three weeks. [70] Several letters were dated on consecutive days as he had to break off writing them. One such recounted the shelling of Geluwe church tower which was being used by German observers to overlook the infantry lines. Felix and his colleague were asked by the infantry to

> *'worry the place. So we went onto a hill where we got a good view of the Church and got into communication with the battery by lamp signalling. By wonderful luck the fourth round burst right inside the top of the tower which should have seriously upset the Boche observing arrangements.'* [71]

He told his mother on 20th October that they seemed to be *'stampeding the Hun'* and that he was scribbling his note to her in between firing a barrage

23. Geluwe church in 2011. Felix was responsible for shelling the church tower in 1918 which was being used as a German observation post. The range finding was very accurate.

and moving on. The Germans barely had time to shell the British positions before they had to move back. Everybody was willing to go without rest so as to break the Germans, he told his sister, also on 20th:

> *'Must stop war-corresponding now. We have to move.'*

Throughout the advance Felix encountered the sight of thousands of civilians attempting to avoid the fighting. The battle area was crowded with civilians, which was the worst feature of the war just now, he told his father. Most were very brave and greeted the British with enthusiasm after being bombarded by all sides. All said that their treatment by the Germans had got worse and worse; latterly all produce had been taken from them and they were never paid. It was a horrible sight to see German prisoners carrying wounded women on stretchers. [72] He told his mother that *'The country is full of civilians and one sees some very sad sights'*.[73] A Belgian farmer told Felix that while the German officers who were billeted on him behaved themselves, the *'simples soldats'* were *'des broutes'*. Felix reflected that *'simples soldats'* of all nationalities became *'brutes'* as far as other people's property was concerned.[74] He referred to a desire for vengeance on the part of locals

> *'If we did to the Rhinelanders as our friends everywhere here suggest we should outhun the Huns themselves. We are told to do all sorts of horrible things to the "sales voleurs."'* [75]

24. *Photographs taken by Felix Brunner of shelled buildings in Flanders.*

25. A British soldier talks to a Belgian woman driving a cart returning to Courtrai, 18 October 1918.

It was a constant problem to find billets for officers and men and stabling for the horses which pulled the guns, and Felix noted that the gunners and drivers had to spend their time polishing, cleaning and scrubbing guns and harness for parade when they should have been resting, which they had earned and would do them more good. [76] He organised three carts every day to help move *'meubles'* for the civilian population who were drifting back to the villages from the towns to which they had been evacuated by the Germans [77] and, on 8th November told his sister that it was *'very hard not to think about peace'* and that hostilities may have abated before the letter reached her.

On 11th November 1918 Felix wrote a long letter to his father, recounting how he and the men he commanded had heard of the Armistice, along with some of his own reflections. People had suspected that hostilities would cease the previous night as they had received conflicting orders to fight a battle but were then told to stay where they were billeted. That morning though, they were told that hostilities were to cease at 11am. The battery cheered when told of the armistice but the news was scarcely believable:

'One hardly dare take it for granted that there will be no more fighting.'

Depending on the internal conditions in Germany, he felt that there would be a four or five month wait for demobilization and that

26. Entry of the Allied armies into Brussels, 22 November 1918. King Albert, the Belgian royal family, and the Duke of York, followed by General Plumer and the Allied Staffs.

> *'one will be relieved of a good many anxieties and will be able to take an interest in the future instead of never thinking beyond the following day. It is hard to realise now that nobody is trying to kill one.'*

He went on to remark

> *'One gets quite used to being in a more or less chronic state of fear. During the last month's battle there can hardly have been a single day when I could honestly have said that I hadn't been more or less severely frightened.'*

These comments are one of the few times that Felix, without couching his words in humour or irony, conveys his honest reaction to the fear that can only have been ever present. They are the words of a 21-year-old who had believed that his future probably lay in death on a battlefield. He later remarked to his sister that '*I am now taking some interest in a future life (on this earth) a thing I never did before on principle as you know.*' [78]

Towards the end of the following two weeks Felix was encamped just outside Brussels and a party comprising himself and other officers from the battery went into the city to witness the entry of the King and Queen of Belgium. He told his mother that the crowds were huge and that he *'had a tre-men-dous day.'* He saw the procession from a viewpoint in the *Grande Ma-*

gasin de la Bourse which refused entry to a number of Belgians but *'six officiers anglais got in without any difficulty.'* From here they watched the processions headed by the King and Queen: *'There was of course colossal enthusiasm.'*

Felix and his fellow officers then called on various contacts of the Brunner family including Ernest Solvay, whose company had devised an improved process to produce soda ash which was utilised by Brunner Mond, the business established by Felix's grandfather and Ludwig Mond. M Solvay invited them to a reception at the *Hotel de Ville* where the king was formally welcomed. Felix felt that it was an extraordinary spectacle as there were only about 150 people in the room and *'It seemed quite impertinent for ordinary common-or-garden young British officers to be there at all'* but that that there was nowhere a British officer in Brussels could not go that day. They eventually returned home at 1am: *'Some day!!!!!'* [79] Felix told his sister that he would never forget the experience.[80]

As the advance continued through Belgian a party of officers and men visited the site of the battle of Waterloo. Felix noted that

> *'All the villages are gaily decorated with Belgian and allied flags and there is much smiling & grinning & nodding and raising of hats and Vive les Anglais! It <u>will</u> be different when we cross the frontier.'* [81]

Felix recounted that his company crossed the border on the Spa–Malmedy

27. *A British officer, lying in a captured trench in Oostaverne Wood, (just over Messines Ridge) writes a letter home 11 June 1917.*

28. John Fowler Leece Brunner, Felix's father, who became 2nd baronet on the death of his father in 1919.

29. Lucy Vaughan Morgan Brunner, Felix's mother.

30. Joyce Morgan Brunner, Felix's sister.

31. Mary Hooper, nanny and friend of Felix.

road on 6 December and that there were *'no excitements of any sort…no one was in sight.'* [82] The day before at Spa he saw the *Hotel Brittanique* where the Kaiser abdicated and noted that a number of German officers and soldiers were wandering around the town as the International Armistice Commission was working there. The locals were not so friendly once over the border but he was able to use the *'small Hun dictionary and …grammar'* he had prudently requested of his sister. [83] One of his last comments in the final letter of 8 December to Joyce, was to acknowledge receipt of a turkey for Christmas celebrations.

Family, food, literature and friendship

Felix wrote very fondly to his family throughout his time at war. He often addressed his sister Joyce in a teasing and affectionate manner, calling her *Dear Little Sister* [84], *My Dearest Maxette* [85] (his fellow officers referred to him as Max during this time), *Dear Ole Bill* [86] or *Ma Nichette* [87]. His tone in writing to Joyce was rather more informal than that to his parents, for instance *'how are all the fat-and-olds…?'* [88] His mother was *Dearest* or *Darling Mother* but letters to his father were always addressed to *Dear Father*. Letters to the lady who was his Nanny, Mary Hooper, affectionately thank her for her birthday wishes and his 'warm underthings'. The warmth with which Felix wrote to his mother, father and sister and the references to other family members and friends indicate close and loving relationships within his family. They were certainly dedicated in sending him the necessities as well as some luxuries which made life a little more comfortable whether he was sleeping in an abandoned German pill box, in the basement of a farmhouse or a room in a chateau at divisional HQ.

Shortly after he arrived at the gun lines in early 1917 Felix reported that *'A sad tragedy has occurred to me.'* - his personal kit was lost. He felt that it had probably fallen off the back of the cart bringing it up to the lines, and he asked his mother to supply a light *'hold-all (roll up sort of thing) with spaces for brushes, shaving things etc.'* and in it one hard hair brush, one hard toothbrush, toothpowder, a light shaving glass, nail scissors, a soap case and two towels. [89]

One of Felix's first requests to his mother after he was posted to divisional HQ in July 1917 was for another pair of pince-nez as his current pair had suffered during his time at the Gun Lines. He remarked that his kit was also the worse for wear and he felt *'rather disreputable'* amongst the smart officers at HQ. [90] He told his sister that about 1lb of chocolate a fortnight was the right quantity to send out [91] and he later asked her to organise a replacement cigarette holder from Abdulla's in Bond St. [92] He confessed in the same letter that James Joyce's *Portrait of an Artist of a Young Man* had defeated him. The next day a letter to his mother instructed her that two parcels a week, including fruit, were adequate.

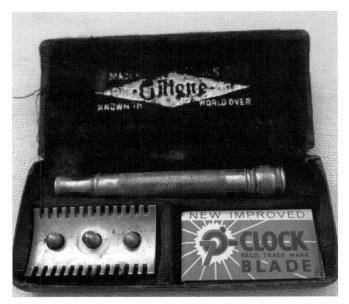

32. A portable razor similar to the Valet Auto Strop razor used by Felix.

Throughout his wartime service Felix's family were assiduous in supplying him with quantities of food including cake, shortbread biscuits, potted meat, a turkey (with carving knife and fork) at Christmas, tinned fruit salad as well as fresh fruit, boxes of apples and Elvas plums, dates and grapes as well as copious amounts of chocolate and coffee. A lot of this bounty was shared around the officers' mess, the fruit salad being *'a top hole sweet for three hungry officers.'* [93] A cake sent by his sister was *'appallingly popular'* [94] and was all gone within 2 days.

Clothing and bedding were other items which were a source of vital interest to Felix. He was very fond of his Jaeger sleeping bag for the colder weather and particularly of his airbed, which was a source of envy amongst his colleagues,[95] and

> *'which has proved a <u>tremendous comfort</u> as we have had nothing softer than wooden 'duckboards' to lie on the last two nights'* [96]

Extra blankets and waterproof [ground]sheets were sent. Field boots and breeches, underclothes (he would send back winter weight items and ask for summer weight replacements) and half a dozen small safety pins for the corners of his collars were requested and provided by his family. [97] Standards had to be maintained and Felix wrote requesting a Valet Auto-Strop razor with four or five dozen blades on 12 June 1918 and by 6 July it was *'V.V.*

33. A Woodbine cigarette packet.

URGENT'. He requested *'a really good magnifying glass for photos, with a fairly large diameter'* [98] which aided analysis of reconnaissance photographs. He had to refuse the offer of a chess board from *Miss Craven*, however, at a time when Felix himself was very occupied when the German Spring Offensive of 1918 looked like it might inflict a serious military setback. [99]

Felix's letters home contained requests for books and magazines as well as comment on what he had just read. He read, and enjoyed, *The Woman in White* by Wilkie Collins in May 1917 but Jane Austen's *Sense and Sensibility* got on his nerves in September of that year due to *'the eternal tea parties and matchmaking'*. [100] He asked Joyce to send him *Anne Veronica* by H G Wells in the 1/- Fisher Unwin edition and also read at various times Henry James' *The Turn of the Screw*, Swinburne's *Introduction to the Works of Shakespeare*, Oscar Wilde's *The Picture of Dorian Grey*, Joseph Conrad's *The Secret Agent*, Tolstoy's *War and Peace* which *'should keep me quiet for a bit'*, [101] George Bernard Shaw, Thomas Burke, Hugh Walpole as well as Rousseau's *The Social Contract*. He also referred to the *New Statesman* several times, to *Punch* and the *Times Literary Supplement* as well as to *Sphere* (an illustrated paper), the *Morning Post* and *The Times* itself. He told his sister that his copy of the paper was destroyed by shelling in January 1918 and in March he referred to *The Times* as *'living up to its reputation as a 3rd edition of the 'Daily Mail' these days'*. [102] (It is interesting to note that Felix found a novelette near an Observation Post in

August 1917 in which the hero was named Daniel Brunner.[103])

In a letter to his former Nanny[104] he told her that he had just distributed 1000 cigarettes (Gold Flakes and Woodbines) and asked her to inform his mother that another 2000 cigarettes and 6 packets of tobacco had arrived that day. In the same letter he asked Nanny to arrange for a similar quantity of cigarettes to arrive by Christmas. The day after the Armistice he placed an order with her for five dozen pairs of socks and gloves and mufflers as

> 'the men frequently sleep in draughty barns where it is almost impossible to get warm'.

He had 63 men in his section who needed these items. Felix commented on the conditions endured by British soldiers and compared them unfavourably to those of German soldiers. He observed that with regard to sleeping arrangements for the rank and file

> 'Their [German] huts are better and are generally fitted with wooden bunks and plentifully provided with wood shavings for bedding. Our unfortunates always have had to sleep on the bare ground or else on wired bunks which are impossibly cold in winter.' [105]

He was quite clear about the privileges afforded by his rank and expressed shame at the contrast between his own and the ordinary soldier's accommo-

34. *Interior of a dugout showing officers of 105th Howitzer battery, 4th Brigade, during the battle of Passchendaele.*

dation in a letter to his father in early 1918:

> '*I have had a comfortable bed & room to myself (not to mention a servant and plenty of kit) and have then had to billet about thirty men in a loft or barn frequently leaky dirty and draughty. The Regular Army is not troubled by thoughts of this kind…*'.

Felix was convinced of the need to recruit civilians whose skills could be of benefit to the army, particularly into supplies, or the Quartermaster role:

> '*a great deal more…would have been done by a really good civilian QMG especially in the direction of improving the conditions of life amongst the rank and file.*' [106]

As an officer Felix Brunner was allocated a 'servant', later known as a 'batman', who acted as a personal assistant, a valet who maintained his uniform and looked after his kit, sometimes cooking his food. Felix had asked for a volunteer from the unit and he felt he had struck lucky as the man had been a hotel valet before the war. He took his servant, Gunner W. Tomlinson 175777, with him from the battery to his new role with the division. Tomlinson exerted some influence it seems as Felix asked his sister to send him a Primus stove:

> '*My servant has ordered me to get one*'. [107]

Tomlinson subsequently told him it worked very well. [108] However in December 1917 Felix explained to his mother that Tomlinson had gone missing and had probably been taken prisoner. Ten days later he had a distracted letter from Tomlinson's mother and Felix asked Mrs Brunner to wire her with any information as those at home could often learn of it before those in the field. He gave Mrs Tomlinson's address in Glasgow. [109] In January 1918 it was confirmed that Tomlinson had indeed been taken prisoner. Felix was pleased with Tomlinson's replacement, Goodall, and in September 1918 asked his mother to supply some tobacco for him as Goodall smoked a pipe.

The living conditions which Felix experienced varied greatly. He was billeted in shelled houses in ruined villages, farms, cellars, the stables of a chateau, a chateau itself as well as dugouts. Later in the war he described one dugout he used as being '*made of an old cellar which has been smashed in on top and reroofed with railway sleepers, corrugated iron and brick rubble.*' [110] On another occasion the dugout measured 6ft x 6ft for '*5 to eat in, 2 to use as an office, and 3 to sleep*'. He noted that washing outside was a bracing experience. [111] Felix moved camp very often and remarked wryly '*Who says this isn't moving warfare*'. [112]

Felix used various methods of transport to move around the area of operations. He often had use of a car, with driver, and described an occasion to his sister during which a shell (*'a projectile from the Baroness'*) burst practically underneath it the effect being to *'lift the front up in the air which banging down again broke the springs and shifted the axle...the driver confessed he was weak below the knees...'*.[113] Felix confided to his father that horseback was not his favourite method as one could not dismount and take cover quickly enough when shelling started and horses were too nervous to take right up to the front line.[114] He also persuaded a despatch rider to show him how to ride a Triumph motor bike which he very much enjoyed learning to use.[115] He did go up to the lines on a motor bike which proved unreliable, however, and required tinkering with to get it to start again.[116]

Standards were maintained in the officer's mess and shortly before the end of the German Spring Offensive of 1918 Felix and his fellow officers shared the benefit of hearing the cheerful tunes played by the small orchestra located outside the divisional commander's mess at dinner.[117] Felix later told his sister, however, that the day after – the orchestra had played *'Bubbly'* and *'Round the Map'* – they had to swiftly retreat: *'a strategic advance to the rear'*.[118] He later rather hauntingly described *'smoking at ease after a most excellent dinner to watch the flashes of the guns and the lights going up from the front lines'* whilst sitting on a restaurant balcony.[119]

Felix was often not able to provide much detail of his work as an Intelligence Officer due to censorship or the sensitive nature of his day to day role so letters to his family often chat about the social life he was now able to enjoy in his time off duty, as well as interaction with his fellow officers in the mess, which occasionally touched on political matters. In September 1917 Felix wrote to his mother that he felt that the standard of intellect in the officer's mess was very strong. The son of the late Chief Justice of Ireland was a fellow officer, 'Lyon' attained a first in Greats at Oxford and the padre was a don at Caius College, Cambridge.[120] (The padre referred to was Joseph Hunkin, later Bishop of Truro, who Felix felt was extraordinarily brave as he always went into battle with the infantry even though he was an artillery padre.) Not long after the taking of Messines Ridge in June 1917 he talked with some officers from New Zealand and Canada who were pessimistic, but prescient, about the future of Europe after the war, and felt that not enough had been done to help the colonies in the past, particularly with capital for their development.[121]

During off duty periods in the mess debates were had about the course of the war:

'we decided... that the idea that Germany would start preparing for another war if we did not beat them was rot. In other words that militarism was dead and damned whether we had peace tomorrow or prolonged the war further', [122] perhaps a less prescient conclusion.

Felix discussed political matters in his letters with his family as well. He deplored that no political party had produced any post war plans and believed that one could not ask people to join a party which had no policy other than winning the war. People who stirred up party faction were contemptible:

'One thing I feel quite sure of, and that is that people who concern themselves with party politics at this of all times in the history of the war, are doing so for the last time... They will never be trusted again' [123] and Felix believed that 95% of the army felt the same.

Felix and his father, who was Liberal MP for Northwich at the time, discussed the prospects of the Labour party as Felix noted that the *New Statesman* was of the view that Labour would do well at the next election. He felt that having withdrawn from the party truce, Labour would have an advantage over other candidates. He could not see a role for the Liberal party after the war if Labour did win support as 'won't Liberalism tend to become merely a compromise?' [124]

This view appears to have been tempered somewhat by the end of the year as Felix told his father that he felt that although Labour was attracting a more highly educated type of man than before, it was unlikely that Labour would 'make any sort of show in the coming election as they appear to have practically no candidates of any reputation' and repeated his view that a programme of reconstructive measures was essential for any party in order to win support. [125]

Relationships developed in the intense atmosphere of battle and within the officer's mess must have been vital and sustaining. Felix vividly described some of his fellow officers such as

'Horace... [who] looks very young for his 23 years, has a simple mind and rather a baby face. He is a tremendous amorist, and spends most of his time writing to girls especially to one to whom he says he is engaged (the others being in support and reserve). He threatens to get married on his next leave.'

He also discussed a colleague called Rhodes who was 'now generally known as Bacchus on account of his somewhat rotund figure and slightly reddish face.'[126]

Felix spoke of Major Ball[127] as 'a nice fellow extremely keen and fearfully energetic...not more than 25...almost brutally tactless' and a subaltern called Downs, 'a large very cheerful youth with a strong Yorkshire accent... from Bradford [and] is about 20'[128] who perhaps reflected the fact that well-spoken regular army types were by now in short supply.

These men and others such as Lyon (a Staff Captain), Thomson ('Tommy' the Brigade Major), Cunnison ('Cunny' a Staff Captain), Green ('Father' or

'Sigs' a Signals officer), Craib (a South African and the Divisional Trench Mortar Officer), as well as the other subalterns with whom Felix served such as Lieutenants Radford, Dean and Johnston with 112th battery and Lieutenants Kershaw, Webb and Watson with 460th battery, were all mentioned frequently by Felix as colleagues and friends. He kept in touch with their frequent postings around the area of combat and they would socialise together when they could in forays behind the lines into the local towns or by simply enjoying themselves bathing in a canal after hot and muggy weather.[129] Felix describes hitting golf balls at the gun lines with the General (probably Edward Hall Stevenson) who had brought some clubs with him:

'I hit several quite good shots to my surprise which rather impressed the General who is a fairly good player, handicap about 4.'[130]

The mutual support provided by such relationships between officers of different social backgrounds and military status was invaluable at the time and was continued by Felix post war.

Felix Brunner spent just over two formative years of his life on the battlefields of Flanders and he chronicled some of the terrible things he saw there in terms which could be starkly vivid, but which were more often masked with humour in order to shield those he loved from the reality. They in turn expressed their love and concern by providing him as far as they could with some of the comforts which might make his daily life a little easier. His family attest that Felix rarely spoke to them of his experiences as a young man at war although his wife remembered his nightmares. In typically understated words Felix Brunner felt that

'One has had many unforgettable experiences, some of them rather painful.'[131]

Coda

The following description of being under artillery fire during the Great War may serve to illuminate the experience of Felix Brunner, although he never described such an ordeal to his family in his letters.

Patrick Campbell was a young artillery officer who was posted to France in the same month as Felix in 1917. He fought in the battle of Passchendaele and recounted what happened to him after taking part in an unsuccessful attempt to break the German line:

'...the shelling suddenly became worse... 'I don't like this, we'd better get down,' Vernon said. But there was no place to get down in... There was a trench at the side of the pill-boxes, but it was so wide and shallow that it was almost useless for protection. But in one place there was a low wall beside the trench... we made our way to it quickly.

I hoped [the shelling] would only last for five or ten minutes, concentrated shelling was usually over in a short time. But it went on. Some of the shells fell very close, and they were big ones. I flattened myself against the earth and the wall. The dressing station was about twenty yards from me, on my right, I was the nearest one to it. There was not room inside for all the wounded men who had been brought there. Some had to be left outside, or were taken outside if they were hopeless cases. They were a long time dying. Unconscious they may have been, but they heard the shells coming. Their crying rose to a scream as they heard the sound of one coming, then fell away to a moan after the shell burst.

I learnt to distinguish the different crying voices. Sometimes one stopped and did not start again. It was a relief when this happened, the pain of the crying was unendurable. But there were new voices. The crying never stopped. The shelling never stopped.

Then I stopped noticing the crying voices. I was conscious only of my own misery. I lost all count of the shells and all count of time. There was no past to remember or future to think about. Only the present. The present agony of waiting, waiting for the shell that was coming to destroy us, waiting to die... None of us spoke. I had shut my eyes, I saw nothing. But I could not shut my ears, I heard everything, the screaming of shells, the screams of pain, the terrifying explosions, the vicious fragments of iron rushing downwards, biting deeply into the earth all around us.

I could not move, I had lost all power over my limbs. My heart throbbed, my face was burning, my throat was parched. I wanted a drink, there was lime juice in my water-bottle on my back, but I could not move my arm to pull it towards me. I could think of nothing but my own suffering. Still the cruel shells screamed down in their fiendish joy, still the sun beat down on us.

It stopped. [132]

Courtesy Percy Campbell

THE REST OF THE STORY

THE soldier returned from the war to the family home at 43 Harrington Gardens, South Kensington. He had been born close by at 23 Wetherby Gardens on 13 October 1897. In a fragment of autobiography, he wrote that he and only sibling Joyce (nearly three years older than him), as small children 'spent most of the time with Nannie [Mary Hooper] being pushed or walked up Gloucester Road to Kensington Gardens. We were devoted to Nannie whose home was in Devonshire, as also was Galliford's the coachman. Together with Mrs Fry the cook they were the mainstay of the family'. Mary (1862-1937) was indeed a mainstay, from at least 1901 until the 1930s. She will have witnessed the death of Felix's sister Katharine, who died in her first year of life in 1905, and seen Felix off to the Western Front. During his service there she wrote to him regularly and supplied him, for example, with cigarettes and 'underthings'. Having been born at North Tawton she returned there to retire. She was affectionately known to Joyce and Felix as 'The Hoopoo' or 'The Hoops'.

Most of his Brunner relations lived in the north, but many of his mother's family, the Vaughan Morgans, lived in London. They were a large Breconshire family who did well in the city of London, and who, some said, were drawn on by John Galsworthy for his *The Forsyte Saga*. Felix's Vaughan Morgan grandfather, Octavius, sat on the Liberal benches in Parliament with his Brunner grandfather which, he supposed, was how his parents met.

From Wetherby Gardens he was sent in 1905 to Warren Hill Preparatory School, Eastbourne. In 1909, the year in which the family moved to Harrington Gardens, he was taken home for health reasons and was tutored by a Mr Thompson. He started at Cheltenham College in September 1912.

One of his friends at Cheltenham was Maurice Bowra, later Sir Maurice, classical scholar and Vice-Chancellor of the University of Oxford. In his book, *Memories* (1966) Bowra asserted that Felix 'disliked Cheltenham as much as I did'. They and another friend 'discovered that by taking walks outside the usual range we could get excellent teas with boiled eggs at farmhouses in the country, and this we did on Sunday afternoons in defiance of rules'. Bowra visited Felix's family in Cheshire and London, and they corresponded while they served in the same regiment at different places on the Western Front.

Felix read Modern History at Oxford and took what was known as a 'War Degree' in 1921: everyone was encouraged to cut their time at the university to free up space for all the ex-servicemen coming through, and most students were equally keen to graduate and get on with their lives. On graduation he joined Brunner Mond in Northwich where presumably he lived at the local family home, Sandiway House, Hartford. But, as his letters from the front indicate, he was interested in political issues and followed the family commitment to the Liberal Party, in particular its Radical wing, of which his grandfather had been a leader. The party had done extremely badly in the election of December 1918, for which it had split into two. Felix's father, John, lost his seat at Northwich, having sided with the Independent Liberals, led by Asquith, rather than with the Liberals who fought the election as members of Lloyd George's coalition with the Conservatives. They both worked for the successful Labour candidate in a by-election in Widnes in August 1919, which the Asquithian Liberals did not contest. At short notice Felix fought the Hulme Division of Manchester in the general election of 1924. In the previous year Felix the Cat had made his first appearance as a cartoon character: photographs from the campaign show a stuffed-toy version of the celebrated animal accompanying the Liberal candidate as his

1. *Felix Brunner and Felix the Cat.*

2. The wedding of Felix and Elizabeth Irving, July 1926.

mascot. The cat was deployed on posters and lapel badges too but it failed to win him the seat. His father lost his in Southport.

1924 was a notable year for Felix in other respects. In May his sister Joyce married William Worsley*. And during the year he met Elizabeth Irving, granddaughter of the great Victorian actor, Sir Henry Irving, and herself an actor. Their paths crossed at the Chelsea home of Frederick Maugham, a lawyer (later Lord Chancellor), who had been at Trinity Hall, Cambridge

---

* Col. Sir William Arthington Worsley, 4th Bart (1890-1973), was wounded and captured on 30 October 1914 while serving as a lieutenant with the second battalion of the Yorkshire Regiment, in the First Battle of Ypres, thereafter spending four years as a prisoner of war. He also served at the beginning of the Second World War. He captained Yorkshire at cricket (1928-9) and was president of the MCC (1961-2). It was said of him by the Yorkshire professional Emmott Robinson that he 'was much too nice a man to play first class cricket' (N G Wykes, *A Memoir*, privately printed, 1981, p. 21). He and Joyce lived at Hovingham Hall, North Yorkshire and had four children.

with Felix's father, and his wife Eleanor (Nellie), a family friend of the Irving's. In January 1926 Felix proposed to Elizabeth at the Royal Artillery war memorial at Hyde Park Corner. They were married at St Margaret's Church, Westminster, on 8 July. By then Felix had become a director of Brunner Mond, a short-lived appointment because before the end of the year the company merged with three others to form ICI. His father joined the board but soon left the company, as did Felix. This severance followed and was largely brought about by an horrific incident. On the night of 3 November his uncle Roscoe Brunner, chairman of Brunner Mond from 1918, and his wife Ethel were found dead in their daughter's house in London. He had shot her with a pistol and turned it on himself. The roots of the tragedy lay in a long dispute between Brunner Mond and its largest customer Lever Brothers; it ended in disgrace for and a financial blow to the former. The story is told by Reader. [1] For Felix and the Brunner family, and perhaps especially for Elizabeth, then pregnant with her first child, this must have been a deeply shocking experience.

Much of the family interest in the chemical business became the founding capital of the Brunner Investment Trust which still exists as a company quoted on the London Stock Exchange. Felix became a director of this and other companies, some in coal-mining derived from Brunner Mond but including engineering, textile and property businesses.

Felix contested the Chippenham division of Wiltshire in the 1929 general election, and came a good second to the Conservative candidate. His father had fought Cheltenham in a by-election the previous year, also coming second. He was re-adopted but he became seriously ill, and died in January of the following year. Felix inherited his baronetcy.

During the Second World War Felix served in the local battalion of the Home Guard in Henley-on-Thames, having moved to nearby Greys Court with his wife and four sons in 1937. He was also an ARP warden in London.

Felix contested the general election of 1945 in the Northwich constituency for which he had been adopted in August 1937. He fought it on the basis of the slogan 'If you want Beveridge [a welfare state] vote Brunner'. The election swept Labour to power and Felix was a distant third. But he remained a committed Liberal and served as president of the Liberal Party Organisation in 1962/3.

Before the war ended in 1945, Felix had taken on the chairmanship of a Unitarian girls' school in London, Channing School, to which he was also a significant benefactor. He remained chairman until 1969. Unitarianism was a commitment he inherited from his grandfather and father. While he lived

3. Felix at the opening of the pit baths Madeley Colliery, Staffordshire 15 December 1934.

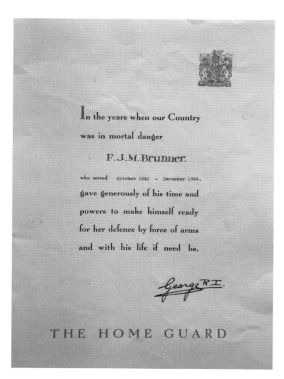

In the years when our Country
was in mortal danger

F. J. M. Brunner.

who served   October 1940 - December 1944.

gave generously of his time and
powers to make himself ready
for her defence by force of arms
and with his life if need be.

George R.I.

THE HOME GUARD

4. Felix's Home Guard certificate.

5. *Felix as President of the Liberal Party 1962/3.*

6. *Felix and Elizabeth after ascent of the Allalinhorn, Switzerland, in July 1937.*

7. *Cartoon by Laurence Irving, poking fun at his sister, Elizabeth and brother in law, Felix and their mountaineering adventures.*

in London he worshipped at its Essex Church at Notting Hill Gate, and he served as treasurer of Manchester College (now Harris Manchester), Oxford from 1963 to 1973. But after he moved to Oxfordshire he regularly attended the parish church of Rotherfield Greys.

He was chairman of Henley Rural District Council from 1954 to 1957, and, following in the steps of his father, of the Commons, Open Spaces and Footpaths Society (now the Open Spaces Society) from 1958 to 1970.

His abiding interest was mountaineering, which dated from his time as an undergraduate at Oxford when he started climbing with a guide in the Swiss Alps. He was a proud member of the Monte Rosa branch of the Swiss Alpine Club. He shared his enthusiasm for mountains and hills with his family. He climbed 4,000-metre peaks in the Alps with his wife and with his son Barnabas, and introduced his younger sons Dan and Hugo to guided climbing and to the British hills. He also loved cricket, supported Lancashire and was a member of the MCC.

Felix had a great love of trees and he planted many at Greys. His favourite poem was A E Housman's 'Loveliest of Trees':

> Loveliest of trees, the cherry now
>
> Is hung with bloom along the bough,
>
> And stands about the woodland ride
>
> Wearing white for Eastertide.
>
> Now, of my threescore years and ten,
>
> Twenty will not come again,
>
> And take from seventy springs a score,
>
> It only leaves me fifty more.
>
> And since to look at things in bloom
>
> Fifty springs are little room,
>
> About the woodlands I will go
>
> To see the cherry hung with snow.

Felix and Elizabeth gave Greys Court to the National Trust in 1969. He died on 2 November 1982.

ENDNOTES

The Brunner Family and the Great War

1   WFL Dick, *A Hundred Years of Alkali in Cheshire,* Northwich, p35
2   W J Reader, *Imperial Chemical Industries: A History, vol 1 The Forerunners 1870-1926,* OUP 1970 p 282
3   Speech, as President of the National Liberal Tradition, 35th Annual Meeting, Leeds, 26 Nov 1913. Quoted in Alan Bullock and Maurice Shock, *The Liberal Tradition: from Fox to* Keynes, London, 1956
4   Stephen Koss, *John Brunner: Radical Plutocrat 1842-1919,* Cambridge University Press, 1970, p 277
5   Sir Felix Brunner's introduction to his WW1 letters p 1
6   Reader ibid p 284-5
7   Sir Peter Allen, '*Francis Arthur Freeth. 2 January 1884 – 15 July 1970*', Biogr. Mems Fell. R. Soc. 22, 104–118 (1956) note 38 pg 110
8   Letter to Mrs Lucy Brunner 18/06/1917

Felix Brunner's War

1   *A salient is a piece of ground projecting into enemy lines. It is particularly dangerous for the defenders as the enemy surrounds the area on three sides.*
2   Letter to Felix Brunner's father, John Brunner 06/10/1916
3   London Gazette 8 December 1916 pg. 11975
4   Letter to Felix Brunner's sister, Joyce Brunner 20/12/1916. *Herbert Asquith, second son of the Liberal Prime Minister, served in the Royal Artillery later reaching the rank of Captain. He later published several collections of First World War poetry.*
5   *On 19 January a huge explosion occurred at the family owned Brunner Mond explosives works at Sivertown in east London which killed 73 people and injured over 400. Censorship prohibited any discussion of it in Felix's letters.*
6   Letter to Felix Brunner's mother, Mrs Lucy Brunner 10/01/1917
7   Letter from Sir Luke Fildes dated 26/04/1917 to Felix's father.
8   Letter to John Brunner 03/04/1917
9   Letter from Norman Hillson 27/03/1969
10 Letter to Joyce Brunner 04/04/1917
11 Letter to Mrs Brunner 05/04/1917
12 Letter to Joyce Brunner 09/07/1917
13 National Archives (after NA) ref WO 95/2234/1_2 pg. 22
14 Letter to John Brunner 11/04/1917
15 Letter to John Brunner 18/04/1917
16 Letter to Mrs Brunner 21/04/1917
17 Letter to Joyce Brunner 24/04/1917
18 Letter to Joyce Brunner 02/05/1917

19 Letter to Mrs Brunner 28/05/17 and John Brunner 30/05/1917

20 Letter to Joyce Brunner 19/05/1917

21 *Two mines were left unexploded, one of which detonated in 1955 when lightning struck a pylon positioned above it, killing some cows. The other remains buried, still packed with explosives.*

22 Aubrey Wade *Gunner on the Western Front* pg. 50

23 NA ref WO 95/2234/1_2 pg. 30

24 Felix Brunner's Commentary on his letters

25 Quoted by Sir Hugo Brunner in his account of his father's wartime service.

26 Ibid.

27 Letter to John Brunner 15/06/1917 *Also noted in the war diary pg. 31 (see endnote 23 for ref)*

28 Letter to John Brunner 30/06/1917

29 Letter to John Brunner 06/07/1917

30 Letter to John Brunner 17/10/1917. *The officer killed was Lt Harold Thompson*

31 Letter to Joyce Brunner 09/07/1917

32 Letter to Mrs Brunner 28/05/1917 and John Brunner 02/06/1917

33 Letter to John Brunner 01/08/1917

34 Letter to Joyce Brunner 24/09/1917

35 Letter to Mrs Brunner 20/10/1917

36 Letter to Joyce Brunner 09/11/1917 *Laurence Joscelyne was 19 and about to take his first home leave when he was killed by a bomb dropped from a plane. He was awarded the Military Cross shortly after his death.*

37 Letter to Mrs Brunner 24/06/1918. *Charles Taylor, later Head Gardener at Greys Court, fought at Passchendaele. Felix and Charles bonded over their memories, although they did not meet at the time.*

38 Letter to Joyce Brunner 20/11/1917

39 Letter dated 01/12/1917

40 Letter to Mrs Brunner 16/01/1918

41 Letters to Joyce Brunner 19/04/1918, 31/05/1918, 25/08/1918; Mrs Brunner 06/06/1918, 22/06/1918, 07/08/1918

42 https://encyclopedia.1914-1918-online.net/article/soldiers_on_leave

43 Letter to Joyce Brunner 06/07/1918

44 Letter to John Brunner 13/10/1918

45 October 1916; March 1917; August 1917; December 1917/January 1918; September 1918

46 Letter to Mrs Brunner 28/06/1918

47 Letter to John Brunner 23/06/1917

48 Letter to Mrs Brunner 14/10/1917

49 Letter to Joyce Brunner 03/05/1918

50 Letter to Joyce Brunner 19/04/1918

51 Letter to Joyce Brunner 10/07/1918

52 Letter to Mrs Brunner 02/03/1918

53 Letter to Joyce Brunner 23/02/1918

54 Letter to Mrs Brunner 24/06/1918

55 Letter to Mrs Brunner 02/03/1918

56 Letter to John Brunner 05/04/1918

57 Letter to Mrs Brunner 14/04/1918

58 *Bowra, later Sir Maurice, English scholar and literary critic, later Vice Chancellor of Oxford University*

59 Letter to Mrs Brunner 21/04/1918

60 Letter to John Brunner 28/04/1918

61 Letter to John Brunner 14/06/1918

62 Letter to John Brunner 14/08/1918

63 Letter to Mrs Brunner 15/08/1918

64 Letter to Joyce Brunner 16/08/1918

65 *The Trench Detectives* Yap Films Series 2 Episode 3

66   Letter to John Brunner 29/09/1918

67   NA WO 95/2291/2_3 pg. 129

68   Letter to Joyce Brunner 30/09/1918

69   Letter to Mrs Brunner 13/10/1918

70   Letter to Mrs Brunner 25/10/1918 *See* P J Campbell *In the Cannon's Mouth p 14-18 for a similar account*

71   Letter to John Brunner dated 04/10/1918 & 09/10/1918 *In 2011 Felix's son, Hugo, visited the church. Photographs inside the church showed that the battery did indeed destroy the steeple while the rest of the building survived.*

72   Letter to John Brunner 22/10/1918

73   Letter to Mrs Brunner 16/10/1918

74   Letter to John Brunner 20/11/1918

75   Letter to Joyce Brunner 15/11/1918

76   Letter to Mrs Brunner 30/10/1918

77   Letter to John Brunner 02/11/1918

78   Letter to Joyce Brunner 15/11/1918

79   Letter to Mrs Brunner 24/11/1918 *The entry into Brussels actually occurred on 22 November 1918*

80   Letter to Joyce Brunner 26/11/1918

81   Letter to Joyce Brunner 26/11/1918

82   Letter to Joyce Brunner 08/12/1918

83   Letter to Joyce Brunner 15/11/1918

84   Letter to Joyce Brunner 18/03/1918

85   Letter to Joyce Brunner 07/02/1918

86   Letter to Joyce Brunner 17/09/1917

87   Letter to Joyce Brunner 09/01/1918

88   Letter to Joyce Brunner 25/02/1918

89   Letter to Mrs Brunner 16/04/1917

90   Letter to Mrs Brunner 08/07/1917

91   Letter to Joyce Brunner 18/07/1917

92   Letter to Joyce Brunner 20/07/1918 *Felix told Joyce that the cigarette holder was made of black vulcanite or ebonite*

93   Letter to Joyce Brunner 05/10/1918

94   Letter to Mrs Brunner 21/04/1917

95   Letter to Mrs Brunner 22/08/1918

96   Letter to John Brunner 08/06/1917

97   Letter to Mrs Brunner 07/08/1918

98   Letter to Joyce Brunner 04/03/1918

99   Letter to Mrs Brunner 09/04/1918

100   Letter to Joyce Brunner 22/09/1917

101   Letter to Joyce Brunner 08/12/1918

102   Letter to John Brunner 27/03/1918

103   Letter to John Brunner 24/08/1917 *Felix and his wife Elizabeth named one of their five sons Daniel*

104   Letter to Mary Hooper 01/12/1918.

105   Letter to Joyce Brunner 27/10/1918

106   Letter to John Brunner 13/02/1918

107   Letter to Joyce Brunner 13/10/1917

108   Letter to Mrs Brunner 25/10/1917

109   Letter to Joyce Brunner 15/12/1917

110   Letter to Mrs Brunner 22/08/1918

111   Letter to Mrs Brunner 22/11/1917

112   Letter to Mrs Brunner 17/11/1917

113 Letter to Joyce Brunner 07/02/1918
114 Letter to John Brunner 24/04/1918
115 Letter to Joyce Brunner 31/05/1918
116 Letter to Mrs Brunner 24/06/1918
117 Letter to John Brunner 24/04/1918
118 Letter to Joyce Brunner 26/04/1918
119 Letter to John Brunner 23/07/1918
120 Letter to Mrs Brunner 20/09/1917
121 Letter to John Brunner 30/06/1917
122 Letter to Joyce Brunner 17/09/1917
123 Letter to Mrs Brunner 09/02/1918
124 Letter to John Brunner 12/07/1918 *In fact Labour did rather better than Felix predicted in the general election of 1918. It greatly increased its vote and became the official opposition.*
125 Letter to John Brunner 30/11/1918
126 Letter to Joyce Brunner 03/04/1918
127 *Major Charles Ball, DSO, MC, after the war became a family friend and business colleague (courtesy Hugo Brunner)*
128 Letter to Joyce Brunner 21/08/1918
129 Letter to Mrs Brunner 18/07/1918
130 Letter to Mrs Brunner 03/08/1918
131 Letter to John Brunner 22/10/1918
132 P J Campbell *In the Cannon's Mouth* p 79-81

The Rest of the Story

1 W J Reader, *Imperial Chemical Industries: A History, vol. 1 The Forerunners 1870-1926,* OUP 1970 pp 371-5

The remainder of this section is based on records held at Greys Court

ACKNOWLEDGEMENTS

The authors would like to thank all those who assisted in the making of this book including staff of the Soldiers of Oxfordshire Museum in Woodstock who allowed us to view and photograph items belonging to Felix Brunner which his family has left in their care. Nick Clarke saved us from committing a blunder by supplying the correct image of the First World War Royal Artillery cap badge with the King's crown on the title page, and Carl Watts of the Green Howards Museum in Richmond, North Yorkshire, provided information about the war service of William Worsley.

Bethany Fisher and Lizzie Champion at Greys Court in Oxfordshire, Felix's later family home, (it now belongs to the National Trust) have been most generous in supplying help and advice. Nick Champion kindly checked the text and his collection of artefacts and documents has been a fascinating and very useful source for images.

FURTHER READING

The Brunner Family and the Great War
A Hundred Years of Alkali in Cheshire, W F L Dick, Northwich 1973
The Escaping Club, A J Evans, Leopold Classic Library (amongst others)
The Silvertown Explosion, Graham Hill & Howard Bloch, The History Press 2003
Sir John Brunner: Radical Plutocrat 1842-1919, Stephen Koss, Cambridge University Press 2008
Imperial Chemical Industries: A History, vol 1 The Forerunners 1870-1926, W J Reader, Oxford University Press 1970
The First Fifty Years of Brunner, Mond and Co, 1873 - 1923, John L Watts, Northwich 1923

Felix Brunner's War
In the Cannon's Mouth, P J Campbell, Hamish Hamilton 1977
Passchendaele: The Story of the Third Battle of Ypres 1917, Lynn Macdonald, Penguin 1978
Gunner on the Western Front, Aubrey Wade, B T Batsford 1959

The Rest of the Story
The Vaughan-Morgans of Glasbury, A Raymond Hawkins, Brecknock Museum Publications n.d.
The Downfall of the Liberal Party 1914-1935, Trevor Wilson, Collins 1966
Child of the Theatre, Elizabeth Brunner, The Perpetua Press 2010

THE BRUNNER FAMILY TREE

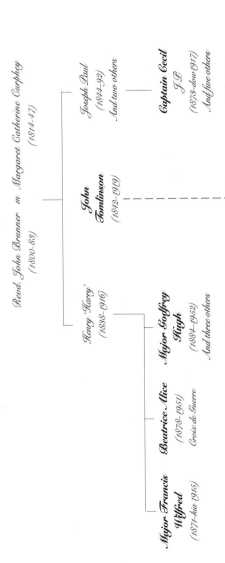

Revd. John Brunner m Margaret Catherine Carphey
(1800-83)   (1814-47)

Henry 'Harry'
(1882-1916)

John
Tomlinson
(1842-1919)

Joseph Paul
(1844-92)
And two others

Major Francis
Wilfred
(1871-kia 1915)

Beatrice Alice
(1873-1951)
Croix de Guerre

Major Godfrey
Hugh
(1884-1952)
And three others

Captain Cecil
J.P.
(1878-dow1917)
And five others

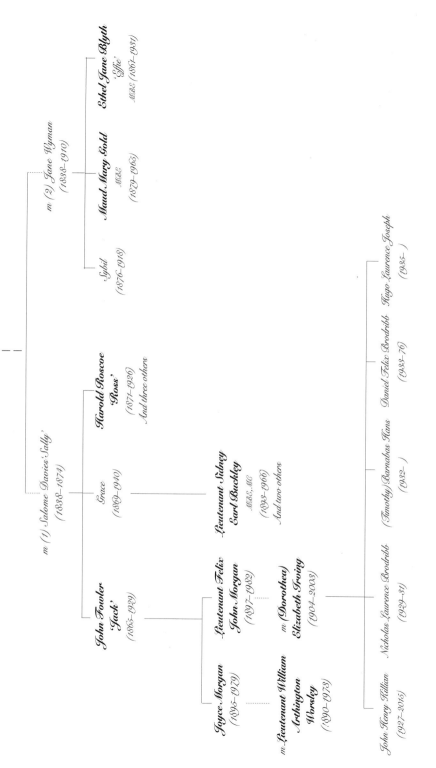